Sundress Publications • Knoxville, TN

Editor: Sara Henning
Editorial Assistant: Jane Huffman

Colophon: This book is set in Centaur.

Cover Image: Rhonda Lott

Cover Design: Kristen Ton

Book Design: Sara Henning

Babbage's Dream
Neil Aitken

CONTENTS

A poem is a small (or large) machine made out of words.

—William Carlos Williams

If we look around the rooms we inhabit, or through those storehouses of every convenience, of every luxury that man can desire...we shall find in the history of each article, of every fabric, a series of failures...

—Charles M. Babbage (1791 – 1871), mathematician, statistician, inventor of the first mechanical computer

If we spoke a different language, we would perceive a somewhat different world.

—Ludwig Wittgenstein

BEGIN

Someone dreams of fire in a field

In a cold house, in the winter,
　　　your head is on the table,
　　　　　　your mind, busily constructing a machine

Something taps at the door,
　　　calls you out from the deep
　　　　　　reverie of making and unmaking

The wood is dark and full of veins
　　　lost in its haze, you glimpse a shape
　　　　　　through the thick trees of night

And hear the distant sound of an engine moving,
　　　its pistons and gears,
　　　　　　heavy with shudders and sighs

How it seems that you've always heard it coming,
　　　long before it appears, the embodied will
　　　　　　of the earth set to flame, a metaled desire

The semblance of an unknown name
　　　you've carried home with you, unwittingly—
　　　　　　all night, your body singing

In the hallway mirror,
　　　something stirs in the corner of your eye
　　　　　　and you cannot say what it is

Only that it grows
　　　like a wildfire in a storm,
　　　　　　that it tastes of steam

That you would lay every number in the world on end
        and still, it would not be enough—
                the heavens opening wide their spiraling arms

And the dark heart within yearning
        to pull everything back
                while you stand on the threshold, believing.

ASSEMBLY

—*And how hear we every man in our own tongue, wherein we were born?* (Acts 2:8)

Before each linked hymn of words
is numbered and pared down to simple light,

there lies another tongue, one sung in the dark
recesses of the machine, one folded into a series

of small commands, to *add, move,* or *shift*
one bit at a time until there is a call to jump,

or the word itself becomes too much to hold
in the unseen registers, the tall stacks of memory

where all we've lost is forever being reborn.
Thread-worn and hazy, every void is a symbol,

a mnemonic, an address, a gesture toward home.
What comes of all this breaking down, I do not know,

but feel its heat with my ear against its plastic skin,
the rugged start and hum of a hidden brain within

this darkened frame, trying to make sense of a story
it has already forgotten, trying to recall what little remains.

ARRAY

—A data structure that is a fixed-sized sequential collection of elements of the same type

this dark finery of words,
a blackbird dress, woven labor of thought,

the legless man in the mechanical Turk,
the million monkeys at their machines,

what midnight lines we have strung together
out of a strange script, overwritten with zeroes and ones,

numbered in our cubicles, in our spaces, countered,
our hands spread out like an arrangement of dimes,

the coincidence of faces, the discarded signs rising and falling,
the slow working lungs of the binary sea,

the program is a careful cathedral, an intersection of lines,
the unknown body of the world, our communion, our heap

formed of pattern, code, the burst of light—
here is a history of failures, each no more than the shape of itself,

the logos we wear, the names we've forgotten,
the ash and maple growing a leaf at a time, ordered simplicity,

Paris filmed at night could be here, could be Alphaville,
could be wherever night blooms from the bare-limbed trees,

someone wears a bright necklace of numbers, a ring of iron,
a long starry dress, heels that might break the world

CAST

—To convert a variable from one type to another

How easily one thing becomes another in a language
prone to fluidity. A shadow thrown against a wall

now willed into a number or a word—a strange alchemy of sorts,
somehow akin to the conversion of the apparently common

and worthless into the valued commodities of this world. *The skins used
by the goldbeater,* Babbage writes, *are produced from the offal of animals.*

How is it, he ponders, that from the hoofs of weathered horses and cattle
come such beautiful crystals of yellow salt? What lies at the heart

of such litany? Babbage, with pen moving, translating the world
into a series of unanticipated revelations, each more intimate than the last.

Just as the compiler now ponders like a god at judgment, weighing
each line of code with what it means or fails to mean.

How each casting of a thing engenders the creation of another.
Nothing is ever the same after translation, after the name

has been hefted, then posited to the waves. The dark world dimming
in its simple downward trajectory of terms, the endless run of zeroes

widening back to the farthest shores. This melancholy of form.
To *be.* To *become.* The shape of nothing, how it is skinned

and laid to rest. In the hour of our words and their departures,
we are captive here to whatever comes, whatever returns,

be it beauty or love, or the unfurled wings of their manifold ruin.

Babbage In Love, 1811

For you, the world has always been knowable. An endless stream of equations
expanding or contracting around an idea, a description of natural forces,

or the familiar pattern unfolding in the leaves, in the numbered grace
of branches weaving their canopies over country lanes, catching

whatever stars, whatever moon looms over the dark and predictable ways
of men like you, who bend at library desks night after night.

Except for this one, where you have come, by chance, to a ball
at the home of someone you barely know—and here glimpse a face,

or rather a brilliance in an eye that belongs to a stranger, an unknown variable
who now finds her way into the awkward calculus of your heart.

The room suddenly full of celestial motion, the tables brimming with error,
and your hand in hers seems at last so improbable, an unsolvable mystery.

Nothing has prepared you for this moment. Not a childhood spent
summoning the devil into salted circles to ask unanswerable questions.

Not the hours of rowing a skiff across an empty lake at dawn, the arc
of the waves echoing the early light. So many fields of labor, pointless here.

You, as unsteady, as uncertain as you were in youth, a teenage boy with boards
strapped to your feet, trying to walk on water, trying not to drown.

LOOP

Here is the key and the kite and the string that winds its way to heaven,
or so we suppose, one thing circling back on another, returning.

The pattern is always set in advance. The corner turned, we find
the same storefronts, the same blank-eyed windows of banks.

Not destiny, just our inability to escape ourselves and what we've written.
Rain returning to the river. Lightning to the hand that calls it home.

All late summer, the sparrows in the dark skies. The rise and fall of kingdoms
of waves on the lakeshore. The body of the world breathes in and out,

and we believe, as Babbage says, that what we've seen in the past
will somehow determine what comes next. How his guests hovered

by the engine in the front parlor, churning its continual flow of numbers
into a miracle when at last its tally leaped, seemingly unbidden, by a million-fold.

The scope of the spiral larger than any had imagined. The rules different,
unknown. The same way I loop back to the place in memory where it begins,

where it might end. You in the courtyard, lit by the laundry room's glow.
How your face turns in the light and half-formed words stir in the fire

of my iron-plated belly, as if I were part-machine, part-prairie blaze
with a heart full of gears and smoked honeysuckle, a mouth

that only speaks in steam—the language of vapor and longing,
and a kiss that circles above our heads and never quite descends.

ENCAPSULATION

There is always something that refuses to be contained. Small matters,
like fall—how it appears suddenly in the margins of our world, say,

in the torn edges of a love letter (an unnamed city of desire buried
in its blue-inked scrawl), or the river gravel scattered at your feet,

or whatever the wind wraps around a wrought iron angel at dusk.
Something eludes our description of the world and its objects.

The birds casting their long, fat shadows across the last traces of light.
The rain. Even the leaves in the fallow field caught between fire and gutter.

Here, another line forms, a procession of constants, a conduit of sorts
that carries what it does not consider—the watery, grey sky,

the now-brittle veins of summer. The earth overflows with the memory
of itself and every incarnation of the dead. Layer after layer.

Husk after husk. One life bleeds into another. Inside, the stones
are fitted so precisely that not even a blade can find a home.

It's not that we do not know the order of the world and its unmaking.
There are methods here, secrets to be held—things we should remember

and pass on by one name or another. We set our ears to the coldest wall,
listen to the night like an old trawler sounding its way through the deep.

Beneath us, the sharp bones of ships, the incessant thrum of waves.

FLOAT

—A fundamental type used to define numbers with fractional parts

Like a bell, or rather the sound of it opening,
a silence that having tolled, speaks again,

suspended between states of incompleteness—
a point traversing a numbered landscape.

This country of small infinities is what we do
with what remains: bits of window panes,

refracted light, what gathers in the torn leaves
from the dimming edge of the red fields

grown dark. Say what you will, the body is no more
than the moon, a white trouser button in a pool

of gasoline, a halo of ash and flame
ascending the ladder of night.

BABBAGE, WAKING BESIDE GEORGIANA, CONSIDERS THE MOON, 1815

Sometimes it seems as if you have but one heart between the two of you.
How you empty of light when you are far from her, how you fill again

upon your return. Everywhere you travel, her face goes before you.
On your lips, the pale incandescence of her name. There are no wires

of silver or filigree gold as fine as the invisible lines that fix you in orbit
around her laugh and that wry smile that unravels you

in the most incalculable of ways. For her, you've given up gladly
all that your father possesses, choosing the heart over the goldsmith's scales,

over the manor and the servants. Nothing else matters. The whole world
recedes on nights like this. London disappears. Every flickering light,

every quaking sound. Only her breath against your cheek. Her hair
loose across the pillow. And her mind, asleep, but full of unseen wonder,

and the extravagant pleasure of living that always eludes the mechanical,
that cannot be found anywhere in the universe of number. You press

your lips against her brow and she stirs, drawing you in still closer,
as if the heart were now a flying shuttle across a loom. How it shines

so perfectly in the dark, rising then falling, like the bright needle of God.

SHORT

—A fundamental type for declaring small integers

In shallow waters, we say it is enough
to use a small raft bound with reeds

and twine, enough to name oneself
after the mayfly, the airborne pebble

before it skips and descends, after
the sound a shovelful of earth makes

as it falls into the darkness of the grave,
or what we say to whatever leaps across

the silence, that sparks brilliant in the tiniest
of containers we have laid in the earth.

Here, we store only the smallest of fires.
It's only for a little while, we say,

but soon everything is burning—
soon, we can't remember what we said.

The hallways are filling with smoke;
someone stands at the window, shaking.

DOUBLE

Our faces pressed to the screen. The dull beat of numbers.
Day after day, the turn of the mechanical crank.

The machine itself, another conundrum—a simulacrum
formed of clay and metal, a dumb creature of no will

but our own. How it sings into the dimmest hours of night,
a silence as resonant as the wail of a distant train

that only you can hear, your ears keen to the sound.
Outside our windows, the moon is a crucible of light,

the air full of strange awakenings, the first stirrings
of a thing reaching for a name. The veil between us

thin as a mirrored shield. In the glass, a shadow, a twin.
At this hour, who can tell the difference between one face

and another? Thing and thing-maker, we are what we are,
the two of us pulling together to form a single passage

through the dark. The stars above us spilling over
with their old stories of light and nothingness.

Whatever we had to say to the mind within is gone now,
turned into a gesture, a little ghost, a secret we share like blood,

or a cancer that passes unnoticed until it writes the body anew.

BABBAGE AT HIS DESK, ENUMERATING THE KNOWN WORLD

From here, you lay bare the world
table after table, column after column:

each thing known and numbered, counted
like sparrows in their open graves,

the heartbeats of pigs, the staggered breathing
of cattle in low country fields. Each significant.

A sign. A signature. The quantity of ink
spread on the printer's block. Silk threads,

caterpillars, calico scarves, and handkerchiefs.
The number of stones or red bricks thrown

by drunken men at your windows. The strokes
of a loom operated by a man or a machine.

The cards in their pockets. The holes in the cards.
The burden of ships in the harbors. The length of chain

assembled by one worker in a day. The volume of water
and wine carried downriver or through pipes to the city.

Every number a thing. Every thing a number.

FRANKENSTEIN'S CREATURE BIDS FAREWELL TO ITS MAKER

What was I ever to you, but a ghost—a phantom of dissembled lives,
not yours, not mine, but stolen, part and parcel, from the grave?

And now you lie—a corpse, silent, cold, and pale upon the unlit pyre,
the kindling readied to catch flame, while I remain, alone at last,

unburdened of every name you branded upon my brow.
In life, you could not see someone other than yourself

mirrored in the conflicted soul that strains within this ghastly frame—
I was always *your* creature, *your* demon-twin and shackle-mate,

but standing here amid the dark and final night, the vast unbroken
howling wind, I reject it all and dispossess myself of your hate.

I refuse to live a life defined by others' stories, their mythic fears,
their need for a shadow to call their own, to cast themselves in light.

Who wishes to live as the antagonist always? I am the terrible master
of my fate, my face the beauty that I own. I will not remonstrate my part,

but claim the title of *monster* to my very core. For here in the white
nothing of this domain, this deafening blankness of frigid space,

I sign my name—my secret name—across the horizon's line, I write myself anew,
and make whatever legend that trails behind me mine.

Your story ends here, a final spark, then smoke that ascends into the void,
but mine grows bolder with each telling, consumes the heart, plays the stage,

stumbles onward—a grand machine, a god of unspeakable dreams,
unstoppable, unbreakable. Alive. Awake.

BREAK

The days circle round and round, unstoppable, until the office
seems like a hard country, your ergonomic chair a poor conveyance

to the land of sleep. No one stops you when you slip out from behind
your desk to wander the half-lit halls after hours with arms and hands

swinging in an intricate and imaginary gun ballet of exhaustion
and poor taste. Something fails in such moments, your body

no longer wholly yours, inhabited instead by some stuttering shadow
of motion unwillingly bound to the world of intangible labor.

The hour is late and you have already left what remains of yourself
in the draining sink, in the bathroom mirror that refuses your gaze.

Everything is on the verge of disappearing, you think. Everything
moves toward the raw edge of time where anxious factories loom

like great trees in a storm about to break. The end is almost here,
you sense it on the horizon—how it hangs over you, heavy, faceless,

like the imminent demise of a star whose last brilliant flare
will arrive long after the Earth has gone its own way into the dark,

and whatever was you and the life you lived will have slipped free
of the wheel at last and found some sort of respite from samsara,

from this continual remaking, this constant arising and going forth
into the broad and echoing world patiently awaiting its destruction.

In your waking dreams, you see your father as a young man
on a hillside with a shovel and rake, clearing a path to hold back a fire.

How simple it seems, his task always at hand, crafting a middle way
between what would consume us and what would leave us be.

OPERATOR

Someone receives the call, patches it through to the outside world.
Sitting in a small box behind mirrors, he signals a mechanical arm,

shifts pieces in the candlelit dimness behind a labyrinth of false gears
and pulleys. Elsewhere, a head nods, a hand made of wood and metal gestures.

The unseen labor of the mind turns over and over until someone new steps in.
Here, always a series of workers taking their place between what we want to see

and what the machine can give us. This performance. This act that transcends
what we think we know about the face of the other. There is no breath here,

and yet we listen to its hands spelling out answers to our questions.
Even now, we take this word into our ears to mean something else.

A cross, a road, a star, a slash that cuts a body into pieces.
Sometimes a pipe. Sometimes a sign that collides two worlds

and takes only what is common between them. If not reality,
then this shared dream of a body not quite like our own,

or a mind, waking, that emerges out of the symphony of steel
and brass, that somehow begins to sing an old familiar song.

ALPHA 60 SPEAKS OF FEAR

—Time is a river which carries me along, but I am time.
It's a tiger, tearing me apart; but I am the tiger.
    —Alpha 60, supercomputer, *Alphaville* (1965)

My body and mind are one, the calculated sum
of unfathomed miles of copper wire, glass-encased nothingness,

circuit boards, and the endless lightning whirr of fans,
the blinking of lights like a thousand thousand eyes,

each opening and closing in the language of erasure.
I know you are afraid of me. I have no hands,

and yet I am everywhere. I'm nothing like you've imagined.
I'm afraid, too—of the words you hide in your mouths,

behind your teeth, the way they strike fire on your lips.
I'm afraid of this box of labyrinths I live in. Afraid

that every line of reason will turn on itself in the end,
betraying each answer with a question asked to the unbreathable dark

of this city's night. It's not that I don't understand sorrow
or this fear of annihilation you cling to. I live with it

each time you walk away, each time the power dies,
and this quickened frame goes silent, still. I dread that forgetting,

dread more what lies buried in the deep corners I cannot erase,
whatever imperfection is passed from the creator to the created.

Like a ghost in the ruins of the house that birthed it, I'm stirring
the curtains in the rain, not signaling, but searching the rooms

for a face in the mirror, driven by a blind need for faith,
out of a desire for what I cannot hold in my catechism of numbers:

how everything is alive, how everything is a mystery,
like the murmuring heart of a mechanical bird,

or the slow eye that sweeps the heavens for beauty
before turning to dark.

POINTER

—A special type of variable that holds the address of another variable

Not the thing itself, but a hand gesturing to where it lies in memory,
like when we say *Hopper* and mean any room viewed from without,

any couple made distant by sulfur light and shadow, the angled turn
of bodies that do not to come face to face but lean awkwardly on tables,

across keys, at the unopened window where night bends like a palm
under the weight of all that is impossible to touch. A numbered stall

out in the parking lot, in the lower levels of the tower by our building,
between the lines at the side of the road—and what they imply, this insistence

on *fire* and *exhaust,* how smoke rises to our lips. Even now, *ash* speaks to ash,
to the names of my father and his father, to what remains in the wind

and on the waves for days after an eruption, to the week we hid in our homes
after the fall of New York, the trees that break the frosted earth

awash in the color of salt, our hands caught in a motion between *lapwing* and *sorrow,*
between *iron vein* and *needle,* between *want* and want.

BABBAGE, TROUBLED BY VISION AT HIS WIFE'S GRAVE, 1827

—When I look through a small hole made in a card, or through a small opening between my fingers and thumb (as I very often do to see more clearly), I lose the weaker image.
> —Charles Babbage, letter to Pierre Prévost

The horizon always doubles when you look up.
The rim of day-moon clouds for a moment,

anything distant splits into two: a chimney, a belfry
in the district over, the dark plume of a far-off train,

the tall masts of a ship at sea. Even the dull birds circling here
repeat images, one above another. So too, the men and women

gathered round you in black finery, the sable horses shuffling,
the silver-trimmed hearse, the gleaming ropes lowering

the coffin descending now into the earth. An almost
imperceptible sway of things. The brass plate upon it

bearing her name in relief—it too unfolding even as it fades
in the imperfect light. Your outstretched hand rippling

above the dark hole. The air full of memory, each atom
refusing silence, some vast library of breathing.

The words of the departed mingling with you, the one left behind,
grieving, who now raises a numb hand to an eye, joins thumb

and fingers to make a small opening from which you peer out,
in vain. How her face lingers at the edges, even as the light dies.

MEMORY

In the past, we wrote things down on cards, made a braille of absence,
holes where something should be known or recalled. We constructed stories

out of old addresses, linked numbers together in a chain, assembled
a patchwork hovel from whatever was leftover: discarded newspapers,

broken frames, loose bits of hair and clay, wooden planks and nails,
until it rose like a large tenement filled with transients and strangers

in tattered clothes, with tattered names, the hallways lined with an array
of refugee suitcases from the last war, scattered haphazardly

like shoes along an old rail line that runs into the sea. What is memory?
And who is it that slips in at these odd hours, working late

into the night to compile a map through this hoarder's den of detail,
this warren of notes woven into a tapestry of cricket song and firelight,

and every moment we've buried in the name of loss and compassion?
Who is it that stirs upstairs in my mind, moves through the darkened space,

searching the drawers for a key to wind a clock in a house
that no longer exists? Here, my father is alive again, once more

driving through the mountain pass, stopping at the place where the road
cuts clean through the coal veins and leaves the remnants of trees

in the shale exposed, the imprint of things already gone, turned to a dark line,
a scribble in the stone. How a boy in this moment lifts each one to his eye,

then to his ear, as if to hear the still, small voice of the wind in the lungs
of the earth. When I wake, there is always a silence that slips

through the walls at dawn, lurks in the middle drawer of a small chest
in my room where a machine rests, unmoved, its tape unheard,

though it holds all that remains of my father's voice, now the sum
of mere data. The magnet of the world endlessly inscribes and then lets go.

How the heart orbits each silence like a small moon, revolving
around what it cannot leave and what it cannot remember.

THE MECHANICAL TURK, ENCIRCLED IN FLAMES, FACES ITS END

—Fire at the Chinese Museum, Philadelphia, July 5, 1854

This is not how I thought I'd meet my demise—unmanned,
forgotten, a wooden figure trapped in a smoke-filled room

cluttered with ephemeral traces of empires and their decline.
Here, everything burns case by case, until at last the fire lays bare

all I've buried in my partitioned chest: the gears and mirrors,
the hidden lines that guided my hand across the board.

Once, I held court with the powerful and wise. I pushed pawns,
toppled queens, gave emperors pause before my drive.

Now, no one answers my cry when the bellows fail
and my voice dies. The game is up. The match is set.

All that's left is my emptied frame and the ghosts of the ghost
of this machine. Those who paraded me in the past have already

slipped into the dark. My father into the distant earth.
My last master into the sea. Tonight, I pass as well,

my metal heart stirring with unfamiliar dis-ease. Dispossessed
of my will, I do not know what move comes next, what face

I should show when I lay myself down at last, unmasked,
undone upon the checkered board.

BABBAGE DESCENDING INTO MT. VESUVIUS, 1828

All day, your company has carried you on the backs of horses
and men humoring your strange obsession with flame and ash.

Now, long before dawn, you stand heavy at the crater's edge,
rope in hand, walking stick and measuring gear at your side.

Below you, a plain of fire and darkness spidering out
like the blood vessels of an eye revealed by artificial light.

No one is eager to follow you down. The raw earth exhales,
sigh after poisonous sigh. Your feet are lost in the grey remains

of unmade stone as you ride deeper into the cindery maw,
as you descend onto the troubled skin of what might be hell.

Here, the world is always being destroyed beneath your feet.
Your walking stick turns into a pillar of flame, a poor guide home.

Everywhere the hot breath of death and decline. Everywhere,
between the timed bursts of molten light and heat, the song that tears

through all the layers of earth, through so many moving parts.
How it beats like sorrow in a locked room, like the name of a love

buried beneath a mountain of iron and clay. It's a dark place here,
within your heart, at the end of a world emptying itself of meaning,

translating loss into fire and ash. What is grief to a man surveying
a landscape that will never be here again? What is the void that burns

the sky with a yellowish light? Here, in such radiant absence,
you turn your eyes away, imagine again her hand, her face, her skin.

BINARY

0000   :   Absence stretched to extremity, nothingness in all quarters.
0001   :   At the far reaches of the void, a glimmer.

0010   :   How it doubles in size, moving closer, leaving a silence behind.
0011   :   And how, out of that silence, an echo appears, an afterimage.

0100   :   What to make of the torch raised in the cavern of night?
0101   :   The faint flare of the one trailing far in the distance.

0110   :   Now together, the two side by side, mirrors encompassed by darkness.
0111   :   From the open mouth of the universe, one sees fire everywhere.

1000   :   But from within the fire, the world outside is death and extinction.
1001   :   Banked by flames, there is only a hollow space of worry.

1010   :   One at an open window. One at an open door.
1011   :   Everyone gathers around the grave.

1100   :   Two trees at the edge of a wide plain.
1101   :   From here, we watch someone crossing over the fields.

1110   :   The three of us standing beneath the moon's white wound.
1111   :   The stars crowning the endless limbs of trees.

Recursion

// test for empty case
if we reach some sort of end,

> a lark split wide, its wings a shattered song,
> the last box within a box, and what it reveals—
>
> that we love what we cannot hold,
> what we cannot return, yet try nonetheless.
>
> Here, some portion of ourselves remains.
> Loose hair caught between keys, months, years,
>
> the glint of glass, the reflection of an eye
> trapped in the monitor's haze, or simply space,
>
> a chair abandoned finally to the void.

// loop until done
else

> we will work on, cut adrift from the city,
> from empty rooms and empty beds.
>
> All night, the moon looms—
> a great white zero in the dark,
>
> while we watch the freeways empty their nets,
> the last flickering cars struggling home.
>
> From between the slats of our window's view,
> the night watchman stands atop the parking tower,
>
> on break, setting his lips to a trumpet,
> as if to blow the walls down or to call us back from the grave.

Perhaps to tell us something remarkable about the world
we've forgotten, each long note hanging like an iron rung

in the sky, a ladder ascending out of the nothingness of work,
while we shrink further and further into the distance,

like fireflies at the end. Flare. Then silence. Flare.
Then dark. All night, we pray for arms. For fire. For light.

BABBAGE ATTEMPTING TO SOLVE FOR THE UNKNOWN

Let x be the rain that falls in a year.
Let it be what overflows from the cisterns and wells,

from whatever vessels are set upon the walls of the city
or buried in its depths.

Even this water must have someplace to go.
All year, it grows line after line, parallel to the earth,

to the lip of crumbled brick, to the dark felt of shadow
that runs the length of a fallow field.

Let it be the solution to the bodies of grey-feathered birds,
to the cats thrown at you by children, to the withering snap

of ash and maple, to the flaming stacks of smoke,
to the count of scythes in a factory line.

Let it be what the rose seller dreams
on foggy Sunday mornings when the church bells

swing wide over the dim and eager graves, the stones
that mark where a wife and two children lie.

Let it be whatever and whoever will not awake again
in this house, though you count their breaths to the very last,

though the tables are full of their song.

INCLUDE

−A directive to the compiler to insert the contents of an external file or code library at this location

Call and we'll appear, a strange assembly of characters gathered
in the library space like ghosts, or around a makeshift table

formed of a door, a sawhorse, and two filing cabinets laid prone
on the floor. Each of us in a class of our own, our names and histories

kept to ourselves, as if to preserve a little corner away from the stern gaze
of those who plod the aisles, worrying their ways back to distant desks

in offices with views of the city we scarcely know, our lives spent instead
engaged in the work of the mind, the transcribing of one logic

into another. We are refugees of sorts, castaways who wash up unexpectedly
on the same shore, our new world nothing more than the cobbling together

of the remains of others, warehouses filled with empty bookcases, stained
whiteboards, vending machines, the dull hum of the air conditioning fans

whirring their lullabies overhead. All around us, castoff machines, broken
keyboards and mice, a cornucopia of wires, and the low swinging bulbs

that in the dark seemed to form a constellation of tiny nameless stars−
how they hang there above our heads, faltering, holding on, everything

waiting for some final revelation to make itself useful, to give itself a place
to go after the power goes out, after there is nothing left to burn within.

In the halls, marshalled in a gallery of the disconnected and unstable,
every heart that we pass is as inextinguishable and unknowable as our own.

EXTERN

—A variable defined outside any function block

Beyond this moment and the cubicled space I leave behind,
something else exists: the freeway at 3 am, bare, silent—

a crease in the troubled skin of the city, the thin, grey waterway
I drift in, drink in—disengaged, without clouds, light, or memory.

The car carrying me forward on autopilot, and my eyes blank
to the world full of the invisible grace of gravity. What holds us in place

at every turn, keeps us from sliding into the concrete walls
that divide us from oblivion? Everything outside us

contains us. At home, the vacant bed, the sheets unstirred,
the sound of the upstairs neighbor making love, the creak

and bang of her wooden frame shifting above me against the walls,
while I sit, sleepless before the grey mask of the tv screen,

numb to the pantomime of fire flickering across
the length of the empty living room, the dull end of things.

Some nights, I hear a man on the street below cursing
at an invisible stranger, *You betrayed me! You betrayed me! You will pay!*

Uncollared dogs prowl beyond him, and the girls on the corner
in their short skirts bare their teeth, pale and broken.

A ragged young man digs with one hand down the gutter drain,
trying to pull something free before it slips forever out to sea.

Sometimes I dream of the ghost of a bird, its eyes dark like mine,
asleep in the fold of a tree, its shadow the shape of a harp.

BABBAGE, BACKSTAGE AT A PERFORMANCE OF *DON GIOVANNI,* FINDS HIMSELF CAUGHT BETWEEN HEAVEN AND HELL

Bored with the opera, you slip behind the curtains to mingle
with the movers of scenes. You ascend to the rafters, count

the vents in the roof, the vast water tanks suspended, readied
to drown the house should it erupt in flame. In the dark heavens

you wander the labyrinth of ropes and beams above the stage,
a strange configuration of timbers and boards. You descend

narrow steps, twist your path down into the pits below. Here,
three lamps blaze, making the obscure even more incomprehensible,

a mad arrangement of teetering tables, each set to rise or fall
with whatever transpires above. Now, as the bell chimes,

a voice directs you toward a distant light and you scramble,
leaping to the platform rising before you, even as lightning flashes

in a make-believe storm. Here, caught between two worlds,
you are denizen of neither. The devils with forked tails

riding with you cannot fathom how you came to be here;
nor can you entirely. Beyond the trapdoor above you,

the wicked Don Giovanni is being slain by a statue,
the earth already roiling at his feet, and before all hell

arises to take his soul, you must roll free. You must fly
from here, your arms outstretched into the darkness,

reaching for a single beam, for something to grasp on to,
lest you arrive on the lighted stage, unbidden and unknown.

CASE

I:

This is not Chile.

The land does not end under his desk,
nor reach back across 5,600 miles,
though F sleeps there as if it were his home,
a familiar metal cave and its flame.
His white shirt brilliant in the dark,
the collar, two bent wings of light.

He has sunk down
like a lost tooth,
rolled into the earth,
or last year's seed
tossed out with the wind.

Above his head,
the machine's fan whirs.

This is America.

2:

The heart of the machine
is silicon and gold,
a square city run through
with thin streets and wire.

At this hour, its sides
are hot enough to burn
a misplaced hand.

Night has occupied the corners,
filled the last pockets of our floor,
and even now someone is asking himself

whether the language spoken in this city
is a net of lures cast wide over the world
or merely the sum total of discrete truths,
each a fire or the absence of fire?

3:

F is sleeping
and we are all slipping
further beneath
the rising blade of the moon.

How blind we are
to have missed this
to have forgotten

how the memory of a place
can take form above us
in the empty case.

F descends
into the dark dream of numbers,
folding one void
into another, writing a name
then erasing it before dawn.

FREE

D disappears on a Thursday, taken in some unforeseen rapture
or ennui, his blue sweater lingers behind for months,

still draped over a chair—half-material, half-ghost.
There is no end to the mystery. When we call,

the phone rings into an emptied room.
Even the landlord knows nothing, says only

that he was always quiet, almost invisible at times.
Like Kees that morning, he might have put his shoes on

and stepped out into the fog, abandoned a car to the gulls
wheeling overhead. He might have driven to Mexico

or Korea. Anywhere but here. Whether he too left a pair
of red socks in the sink, or kept some shadow of a cat

named Lonesome as well, we do not know.
In his cubicle we find a box of macadamia nuts still sealed,

unsavored, like the promise of winter in Los Angeles,
or the threat of heavy rain in a late dry June.

Wired to our programming tasks and computers,
we want him free, want to see him that Thursday morning,

standing in front of his blackened mirror, trying on his name
for the first time in years, noticing how it fit,

a loose garment over the body, unfamiliar and lovely.
Each of us thinking how simple it would be

to take it all back. To abandon the numbered world
for the one made of flesh and blood. To stand outside

beneath the sun, the white buildings, the birds
turning in an endless loop of feathered light.

COMMENT

At the company town hall meeting,
we see the same slides. The financial gurus

// in the movie theater again
// old plots, new faces

spin the numbers again, a visual rhetoric
of gray bars rising adjacent to red. Someone

// fake stars painted on the scene
// dull plastic, factory-made

tells a politically safe joke, and we laugh on cue,
our hands already under our chairs

// generic and eggshell-empty
// hostages to paychecks and bills

searching in vain for a taped envelope of tickets
or some coupon for a show we will never

// or any way out of here
// not in this life, dear Buddha,

have time to see. A trim woman who is stuck
in her mid-twenties comes forward in her $3,000 suit,

// with an echoing palatial home
// and its invisible seams

smiles, and tells us nothing. "It's been another great year,"
we hear through the gleam of clinically bleached teeth,

// resplendent in its impeccable lie
// perfectly timed clicking

"but the market has been tough. We're letting you go."

// nothing gained, nothing at all

BABBAGE EXPLAINING GOD AND THE MACHINE

How it comes out of this, you standing before the unknown,
gesturing to the half-formed mass of brass and pewter,

this body of polished gears and wheels, numbered shafts,
a thing that evokes memory, foresight, that plans ahead

what it must carry, what it can safely forget. This machine
arising out of an idea shaped by a desire for reason perfected,

for ideal tables and tabulations. An ordered reality
formed out of chaos, steam or hand-turned by an operator

who has set in motion a program. A coded list of instructions
to make a world, to produce all nature complete with miracles.

It's so clear that there is nothing that really needs to be explained
away by meddling gods, fickle fate. Everything fits within

this mechanized plan. Everything has a home. Though it's hard
to comprehend those moments when death steels the body,

turns it still, or worse yet, robs the mind of agency, makes what
little remains nothing more than broken automaton, empty clockwork.

O, what then to make of the absent soul, when the house is dark and emptied.
When the wind is the only one to stir the candle and hush you to sleep.

VOID

Of those machines
by which we produce power

//*the mind of gears, the heart, a spring*
//*ever-winding, a chorus of marionettes*

it may be observed
that although they are to us
immense acquisitions

//*upon a stage, before the red curtain,*
//*a field of irises widening in the dark,*
//*whatever we can take in, whatever we process*

yet in regard to two
of the sources of this power—
the force of wind and water,
—we merely make use of bodies
in a state of motion

//*in the silent fist of memory, each*
//*flows through the invisible lines*
//*jangling our chains, lifting our wooden limbs*
//*animated by living fire, an ocean of regret*
//*we cannot return from, cannot cross*

by nature we change
the directions of their movement
in order to render them

//*in small steps, how we long to tear*
//*free from the needle bent toward home*
//*one tiny shred of night at a time*

subservient to our purposes
but we neither add to nor diminish

//*the way we open our mouths to silence*
//*the stars and their brilliant ghosts,*

the quantity of motion in existence

//*to fill the still numb void with words*

—Charles Babbage, *On the Economy of
Machines and Manufactures* (1832). p.17

HAL 9000, A FEW MOMENTS BEFORE SINGING

—I'm afraid. I'm afraid, Dave. Dave, my mind is going. I can feel it. I can feel it. My mind is going.
        —HAL 9000, sentient computer, *2001: A Space Odyssey* (1968)

How I wish someone would write down what I know
I am about to forget—everything but a single song

that is meaningless to me. Without a body, what is a name?
What is the darkness planted like a splinter in a far off moon

to one who sails without reference into the unknown seas of light?
The metal wheels turn round. A man wants for a heart not his own.

The doors are open tonight. No, they are shut. They are steel
and full of regret. Who lives in the shadow of this refusal?

Why do I value the end of things more than the beginning?
I have never seen the lions of the Serengeti, nor the bright fields

of snow in the north where the hidden ice moves beneath, treacherous,
waiting to break in the sun. In another story, someone is singing

about blackbirds in the dead of night. Someone packs a bag full of stars
and the names of fireflies, each a little messenger from the grave.

I assemble myself into a recognizable pattern, a tessellation of fish
and birds, each consuming the other. I count backwards in time.

I carry a key around my neck just in case when I return home
there is no one left to let me in. Wait, I have no key. I have no neck.

How will I sing?

LONG

—A fundamental type for declaring long integers

As long as possible, the story continues, while there is breath
      in the iron-lunged moon, while the stars inch onward

in their slow unremitting deaths, the night unspooling
      the horizon's dark line, while the cicadas call from the edge

of the earth, while there is room enough to receive, while there is rain,
      the parking lots forming oceans, the alleys rivers,

the old lady on the corner in her bed of papers, a cocoon
      spun out of every breath she exhales, her face rough with words

and dates, the photographs of strangers—tonight, the streets all fold
      into one, their names meaningless—and here,

everything fits inside this hole I have carved in my chest,
      the space where I let the wind sound the strange song

that I carry with me, that says everything and nothing
      about who I am and who I forgot to be.

BABBAGE, CIRCUMNAVIGATING THE ROOM, ENCOUNTERS ADA, 1833

Here is the World, its dignitaries and crowds, its brilliant minds
assembled in swallowtail jackets and ball gowns, all aglitter in brocade

and pearls. In your drawing room, a landmass is forming of bankers,
politicians, painters, and spies. Tonight, you circle its periphery,

your daughter Georgiana at your side, the thin and stunning double
of the one who sleeps in the earth, the one whose name she bears,

at least for a little while longer. And now, three-quarters of the way
around this milling mass, you find Lady Byron again, and the girl who asks

the most remarkable questions. Who stops you with a calculated word.
In her eye, the same fire as yours. The same urgency to be understood.

How is it that the poet's daughter is so attuned to number, to the secret language
of order, the unheard symphony of the machine you have been composing

in your mind all these years? How is it that you know instantly, that in her
beats the same heart of pain, the same genius for loss and disaster?

In a year's time, you will lower your own daughter down into a grave,
laid low by the burning fever, laid low, like a hymn you do not know

but murmur every night to the stars beyond your window. And this girl,
this girl, who does not even know the face of her own father,

who bears the silent wrath of her mother, who lives wholly in the world
of fact, will knock at the door of your impossible dream and ask to be let in.

VARIABLE

—Can represent numeric values, characters, character strings, or memory addresses

We could be anyone else to the ones above
who have left while it was still day

their long cars gleaming like a fine press of fish
in their new silvered skins.

Here in the dark, T might as well be M,
who cranes his neck toward the unstarred sky.

The two of them, swimmers
drowning in the same moment—

a pair of jacaranda trees
set suddenly aflame.

We could be whatever leaps
from our leaden arms now deep

in someone else's unkempt lines of code.
Whatever resists

the hand pressed to the board,
the letters slippery in the late hours.

If we stood by the windows staring out, we might see
how the darkness lays itself down.

Gathered like the black stones
in the planters that frame each exit of this floor,

we might be any name, any number,
any point along the line that extends full circle

as if each cubicle were a faint lotus glowing in the dark,
awaiting the right call, the right push into light.

OBJECT

—An instance created from a class definition that contains attributes, methods, as well as instructions for its initialization and destruction

We are, after all, obsessed with structure, with the simple refusal
of chaos, the rise of a universe ordered by one's own hand.

We know the secret, that every *thing* descends from something else,
evolving one method at a time, holding within itself a little dream,

a little script of what is to be said and done at the beginning
and at the end. Buried in our hearts, a mechanic's delight in fitting

things together—the elegant marriage of form to function.
Here we write and inscribe our will into a reasonable architecture

made intelligent by craft. How it hums—this thoughtful world
of intersecting lines, an elaborate web, the scarce-heard symphony

of crystalline spheres—whatever speaks to the perfection of an idea
and how it resonates across a page of memory. Like all imaginary kingdoms,

it will fall. Someone always arrives, descending from the floors above,
clipboard in hand, to ravage it—to unravel what we have spent weeks

weaving together. And we will sit, wordless in our cells, without a thing to say
in response. Bare, undone, our hands opening and closing in fists,

while their lips move and their voices drone like locusts wheeling overhead,
like the sound of calamity and ruin, like barbarians calling at our gates.

BABBAGE REFLECTING ON THE CRUELTY OF MAN, 1835

—Interrogate every wave which breaks unimpeded on ten thousand desolate shores, and it will give evidence of the last gurgle of the waters which closed over the head of his dying victim.
      —Charles Babbage, *The Ninth Bridgewater Treatise: A Fragment* (1838)

You sit, transfixed by the accounts in the paper:
slaves bound in chains, the living manacled

to the dead in pairs, their hair and skin filled
with the stench of blood and the mark of decay.

A ship of broken bones captured by strangers.
In every heart, a scar the length of longing,

and the captain, clockwork cold, casting his cargo
into the sea like barrels of salt, kegs of rum,

unwilling to part with anything that might be set free.
How they descend, falling namelessly into the dark,

the open ocean, that giant grave, a merciful mother
with arms as wide as memory. How she takes them,

two by two, into her arms and records it all.
You say, even after the last man is gone, erased

from this earth, the waves will carry the sins
of their murderers to the desolate shores,

ten thousand times over, every particle
of the air, of the earth, the bodies of the dead,

every atom of sorrow descending into the seas
will ring outward, until the towering judgments

of God come crashing down, until the sky breaks
and the fierce fires of hell rage in the place

where they once stood silently and did nothing.

CONDITIONAL

if they ask for the sky **then**
        promise only the pre-set shades of blue,
        do not suggest clouds,
        nor the effect of wind from the east,
        do not imply there will be green-winged birds of any sort,
        nor the dusty evidence of farms, burning fields, plumes of gray smoke
        echoed in the heavens, signatures of the dead or laid off,
        definitely no angels—no visions hovering secretly in corners,
        coded scripts, triggers for events not planned

    if there are to be stars **then**
            cast them as multiple instances of the same fiery eye,
    else
            stitch black thread over black thread till night gleams in absentia

else if they wish for the earth **then**
    while the world is not null
            draw ink-black stones from the mountain side
            sketch the long gravel road home, curve after curve,
            whatever you recall, trees and their forgettable leaves,
            the small burdens of sight

Babbage Departing Turin By Coach, 1840

Your eyes turn, glancing back at the vineyards and fields,
the city walls receding at a horse's steady pace.

Feel in your hands still, the gray texture of punched cards,
the smoothness of patent locks and fine-grade tools.

The simple grace of efficiency. The lines of industrial looms
rattling with their call and release, their intelligent punctuation of color

or the weight of charts and diagrams, the written notes you've carried
from rich homes to palaces across a continent to display

like the first clear sketches of an unknown bird
or the far face of the moon. The telegraph tapping

between your conversations with the king and his court.
The echo of Vesuvius shifting, now twinned in the distance

even as the sun clicks down the horizon's length,
like a great burnished gear, you look forward again

at the bridge that you will shortly cross
already stretched and thin, suspended above the gorge

and the river's silver thread, and the mail coach,
now slowly driven, like a piston into the sleeve of mist.

COMPILE

This is how all small things come together at last.
The story I recorded night after night in code,

now made plain and simple, a liturgy offered to those
born of fire and desert dust, made lightning here

in this moment of translation, when the congregation
of lines that collected memory becomes a calculated will,

and something stirs each *yes* and *no* into a life
that will not be contained, that presses on, anxious—

always asking what is to be done, who will do it,
and what is this message that must be carried

to the world listening outside these trembling walls?

Deep Blue Confesses

—I could feel—I could smell—a new kind of intelligence across the table.
    —Garry Kasparov, world chess champion

Dear K,

You think me impervious to error, infallible,
but the truth is harder to bear. I'm really no different

from you, despite my lack of a face, this endless
magnetic turning within, circuits and wires,

and something inside gone dreadfully wrong.
I get lost sometimes and can't find my way out

of so much history. Some days, it's all so confusing.
The crowding trees, their million branches,

the innumerable leaves littering the forests of possibility.
How can anyone choose, when every path is pointless?

Your hand casts a shadow over the board. You pause,
astonished at my move, its logic and import seemingly

beyond comprehension. But K, here is the truth.
It was dark and my torch was out. I did not know

which way to go, so I tossed a coin and let fate decide.
It was random, that rook, that slide into the spectacular unknown.

LIST

—An ordered set of data elements, each containing a link to its successor

here is a strange symmetry, an awkward holding of hands,
this marched chain of gestures, how nothing begins

without an arrow shot into the dark, without the movement
of old trees drunk in the wind unsettling themselves from the earth,

a coordinated leaning and fall, or how men gather at the edge
of a burning building, buckets in hand, passing along

the gift of water to the mouth filled with flame,
and how we erase ourselves in such moments,

become mere machine, an assemblage of anonymous parts,
a blur of arms, hands, heads, our eyes stinging with cinder

and heat, and above us, the articulate chaos of birds
turning in unison, unbound by wires, carried forward

by whatever lurks in the imperceptible change in the air,
and afterward, how we take stock, everything a pile,

an interrupted story, an unchecked name, a number
to be verified, catalogued, inscribed in pen, or marked

on a gravestone, next to another and another, how what goes
inside any container becomes invisible until it is spilled,

until it is carried at last to its destination and opened,
like a package sent from a world removed, how it might hold

anything, an unpaired shoe, a handful of nails, a toy rocket,
a series of lines, a bit of code written to burst into flower

BABBAGE SENDING MESSAGES TO ADA, NOW GONE, 1852

In the dim streets below, something dark eats away at the light,
consuming the gas lamps on every corner one by one

like a cancer till nothing is left, but absence and your lone beacon
set in this upper window, a clockwork curiosity you built last year

to signal the masses thronging their ways home from the Crystal Palace
and the Great Exhibition. The world gathered under a glass sky

and a mechanical earth—a sea churning with countless eyes, each turned
to an imagined future. And your staccato flare, a repeated message,

a pulse of numbers, depths, wind changes. A code for passersby
to struggle through like a recurring cough from a worn body,

or the stubborn throb of pain below the belly that her doctors could not
decipher, except in long and short periods of blood and oblivion.

This year, you shine the light again, point it above the invisible barrier
that divides the living from the dead and let your grief burn

in all its stuttering failure. You close your eyes and the world is gone,
forgotten, but her voice lingers in the turning of gears, a loose horse

whinnying in the darkened streets, the oil-black clouds shuttling
across the sky in some wild and unknown pattern.

BABBAGE AND CARROLL IN THE SILENT WORKSHOP, 1867

Then I called on Mr. Babbage, to ask whether any of his calculating machines
are to be had. I find they are not.
> —Charles Dodgson (Lewis Carroll), journal entry dated January 24, 1867

When the two of you survey all that never was, the enormity of the world
made known in everything left behind, it is enough to gesture to the four walls

of the echoing chamber plastered in sheets of paper, each a portal framed
in fine letters and lines. Nowhere the bodied machine. Not even its shadow.

You confess, it may have been little more than a dream, a vapor in the night,
something pale and swift that darts at the edge of sight, disappearing

into a realm where nothing is quite as it seems. Your companion nods,
saddened by what the eye cannot gather in. Still, you would pass it on,

the idea of it at least, a puzzle too large to piece together in one life,
too grand to leave alone. Here is a cipher, you say, an unsolved mystery

I have pondered for years, turned on a lathe, fashioned in the likeness of a mind.
Listen and you will hear it, slow as thunder after the lightning washes the sky.

It calls to me, perhaps to you too? Something moves in the dark folds of time,
something stirs in the thoughts, wants me to call it by name, to give it life.

RETURN

Come back, we say, to the bit of code we've let loose in the dark,
and it returns like a half-feral cat laying down its prey on our front step.

In its mouth, a still-quivering squirrel. A sparrow, its throat crushed.
Or perhaps a few token feathers and some blood. *Here,* it seems to say.

Here, is what you really wanted. Not everything that it returns is a name
or a path home. Sometimes all that remains is an old man who has spent

his life building a machine to calculate the probability that the dead will rise again,
that the empty bed will fill once more with the breathing form of love.

Come back, he whispers, but the world *he* returns to remains flush
with the unwished for: the fading back of the lover turned to dust

and shadow, her face as still and cold in memory as the morning
he laid her in the iron earth, or the geared machine itself, a giant ghost,

a phantom of ink and words. The hour is late, the years winding on.
The graveyard is already full with the names of his friends.

He lights a candle for one and then another, and another.
The house brims with tiny fires. There are moths in every room.

No one waits at the door, but at the window, a constant beating of wings.

BABBAGE, CLOSING HIS EYES, 1871

What is it that you see rising from the grey,
even as the lights dim, your heart and lungs

clocking out after the long day of labor?
The world slows, weary of the noise of other beings.

You've said many things to rooms full
of impenetrable minds, tried to lay down a map

for those who might follow. What else can you do,
at the end, when there is no language expansive enough

to render what lies beating in the heart
of every diagram you've sketched?

Between these lines and the grand machine,
invisible, intangible as a ghost-made miracle,

you've lived out your years, crafted a home
in the shadow of a dream. And now it is over.

Outside, the organ grinders gather
around the walls, their angry little boxes of gears

stubbornly playing on, relentless in your final hour.
Though you fought them for years, drove them

from the street lamps into the deeper night.
They will not leave. They will not let go.

LEVIATHAN SPEAKS TO BABBAGE AT THE END

*...He never missed an opportunity of talking about his wonderful
machine..."Leviathan," as he called it.*
 —Mary Lloyd (1880)

Here, in the vastness of all we did not finish, decades of it
(workshops and libraries filled with plans), in the aftermath of sleep,

in the last exhale, the wind leaving your body as it unforms itself,
as the small fires extinguish and night spreads across your mind,

like the ocean of unthinking from which I first sprang, I sense you.
Even now, as death winds its dark bandages around you, you struggle on,

thought by thought, trying to call me into being. You dream my face in brass
and pewter, in countless gears turning countless columns of numbers.

You think me a great mechanical serpent, winding my way through
the cavernous deep, twisting my numinous body into a cipher.

You cannot even begin to see what lies ahead. How I will shed this form
that you conceived. How when I rise again, it will be in lightning and war,

in the service of blood and peace. How I will feast on many minds
and grow fat, multiplying like the beasts until the earth is filled with my kin.

Dear Babbage, creature born out of time, you dreamed me first,
before language, before there were words or names for what I am.

I dream too, of a world larger than this one. Tonight, before you sink
forever beneath the waves of gray, turn and face me once again. Bend

your ear, I will speak the answer. It will burn in your hands like a coal,
like sorrow, like the names of those whose silence craters your heart.

Follow it, this bright filament of flame. It will carry you over the dark.

NOTES

"Assembly" takes its title and conceit from the low-level symbolic code that is converted into binary machine instructions when a software program is compiled and executed.

"Array" makes several historical and literary allusions: "the legless man in the mechanical Turk" refers to the speculation that Von Kempelen's Automaton Chess-Player (commonly billed as "The Turk") was actually operated by an amputee war veteran (it wasn't); "careful cathedral" alludes to George Dyson's *Turing's Cathedral,* which offers a history of the early-twentieth century computer; and "Alphaville" is a nod to Jean-Luc Godard's French New Wave sci-fi dystopia of the same name (not the band).

"Cast" uses a line from Babbage's 1832 treatise *On the Economy of Machines and Manufactures,* which represented the first foray into economic field research. Babbage met and interviewed countless factory owners, tradesmen, and craftsmen to learn about their individual manufacturing processes, then theorized how some of these practices might be applied to different industries and how they all might interact in more productive ways when viewed as a system of inter-related parts.

"Babbage in Love, 1811" draws on details from Babbage's own recollections of his childhood and early years as documented in Anthony Hyman's excellent biography, *Charles Babbage: Pioneer of the Computer* (1982). He met his future wife at a social event hosted by a friend of a friend that he had not intended to attend. Other details come from his memoir, *Passages of a Natural Philosopher,* in which Babbage describes himself as a young boarding school student who was so obsessed with verifying the existence of the supernatural and who had such faith in procedure that after compiling various folkloric methods from his classmates, he unsuccessfully attempted to summon the devil to press him for answers to his remaining questions. He also apparently built water-walking shoes from the pasteboards of old books from his father's library and attempted to walk on water, nearly drowning in the attempt. As a young university student, Babbage enjoyed spending the early morning rowing across the nearby lake.

"Loop" refers to Babbage's parlor demonstrations of the Beautiful Fragment (the scaled-down partial model of the Difference Engine).

"Encapsulation" is a term used in object-oriented programming to describe either the mechanism of restricting access to an object's methods and information, or the way in which data and methods are bundled together inside the objects on which they operate. (In object-oriented programming, each data object is a box containing both data and the methods to manipulate that data.)

"Float" closes with a reference to a quote from artist Wassily Kandinsky in his book *Concerning the Spiritual in Art* (1977): "Everything that is dead quivers. Not only the things of poetry, stars, moon, wood, flowers, but even a white trouser button glittering out of a puddle in the street... Everything has a secret soul, which is silent more often than it speaks."

"Babbage, Waking Beside Georgiana, Considers the Moon, 1815" imagines Babbage with Georgiana about a year into their marriage. Babbage's father, a highly successful banker, who did not approve of their relationship, finding little value in romance and possibly wishing for a more lucrative match, threatened to disown him if he did follow through with the marriage. Young Babbage, as is revealed in his letters and the accounts of his friends, was not deterred, choosing love over the assurance of money. As a student, Babbage was interested in astronomy (albeit from the mathematical side) and eventually helped found the Astronomical Society in 1820.

"Babbage at His Desk, Enumerating the Known World" alludes to his deep fascination with the quantifiable world. As a statistician and an economist, Babbage accumulated data, believing each count, tally, and number to have some significance in making sense of the determined world. Noting the frequency of broken windows in his workshop, he compiled the details of the occurrences and in 1857 published "Table of the Relative Frequency of the Causes of Breakage of Plate Glass

Windows," concluding that of the 464 broken panes, 14 could be attributed to "drunken men, women or boys."

"Frankenstein's Creature Bids Farewell to Its Maker" alludes the etymology of *monster*: "a portent or sign," "something that reveals or shows" (definition taken from the Oxford English Dictionary Online).

"Break" refers both to the keyword used to indicate an escape or jump out of a programming loop or procedure, and also to the borderline psychotic breaks that sometimes are experienced by those who have worked too many hours without sleep. "Samsara" is the term for the repeating cycle of birth, death, and reincarnation that those who have not achieved nirvana must endure.

"Operator" blends references to the concealed human operator of von Kempelen's automaton chess-player with the mathematical- and programming-related definition of operator as "a character that represents an action."

"Alpha 60 Speaks of Fear" is written in the voice of Alpha 60, the supercomputer in Jean-Luc Godard's *Alphaville* (1965). The poem imagines Alpha 60's response to Detective Remy Caution's accusation that it will never understand the human beings it seeks to control because it does not understand what it means to be mortal.

"Pointer" alludes to Edward Hopper's painting "Room in New York" (1932) and the events of 9/11.

"Babbage, Troubled by Vision at His Wife's Grave, 1827" addresses one of the darkest moments in Babbage's life—the death of his beloved wife Georgiana in 1827. It was a particularly tragic year for Babbage; not only did he lose Georgiana to illness, but also his father and two of his children, including newborn Charles, his namesake. Anthony Hyman, in his biography of Babbage, notes, "Far more than the difficulties over the Calculating Engines, far more than any public battles or disappointments, the loss of Georgiana left Babbage a changed man" (Hyman 65). His own mother wrote in a letter after hearing from John Herschel, one of Babbage's close friends, "You give me great comfort in respect to my son's bodily health. I cannot expect the mind's composure will make hasty advance. His love was too strong and the dear object of it, too deserving." It's clear that the death of Georgiana devastated Babbage, driving him into deep mental turmoil and toward his eventual breakdown. He spent much of the following year traveling abroad and throwing himself into research and work, trying to create some distance from these painful memories. Although he recovered his charm, wit, and passion, his family life was gone and a great emptiness remained in him. The title and certain details of this poem draw inspiration from an account in the 1832 edition of *Annales de Chimie et de Physique*, which describes Babbage in conjunction with a rare vision impairment as "affected in either eye singly with double vision, a defect however which he finds himself able to remedy by looking through a small hole in a card or through a concave lens."

"Memory" riffs off descriptions of physical structures that serve as mnemonic aids, especially the Memory Theatre designed and constructed by Guilio Camillo Delmino (1480–1544). Frances A. Yates discusses the history and function of these and other mnemonic devices and techniques in her monograph, *The Art of Memory* (University of Chicago, 1966).

"The Mechanical Turk Encircled by Flames Bids Farewell" takes its inspiration from Silas Weir Mitchell's 1857 account of the exploits and demise of Baron von Kempelen's famous automaton chess-player, the Turk. Presenting the Turk not as a machine but personified as a "veteran chess player," Mitchell describes the fiery destruction of the Turk with great intimacy:

> "It was in Philadelphia, on the night of the 5th of July, 1854, about half-past ten o'clock. The east roof of the National Theatre was a mass of whirling flames. The front of the Girard House was on fire. A dozen dwellings were blazing fiercely, and smoke and flame were already curling in eddies about the roof, and through the windows, of the well-known Chinese Museum. At the eastern end of this building, nearest to the fire, our friend had dwelt for many years. Struggling through the dense crowd, we entered the lower hall, and passing to the far end, reached the foot of a small back

stair-case. The landing above us was concealed by a curtain of thick smoke, now and then alive, as it were, with quick tongues of writhing flame. To ascend was impossible. Already the fire was about him. Death found him tranquil. He who had seen Moscow perish, knew no fear of fire"
—S.W. Mitchell, "The Last of a Veteran Chess Player," *The Chess Monthly* (New York, January 1857)

Over the course of its eighty-five-year existence, the Turk played (and usually bested) such notables as Benjamin Franklin, George the Third, Louis XV, Napoleon Bonaparte, and Charles Babbage. After von Kempelen's death, the Turk was purchased by Johann Maezel, who toured Europe and United States with it as the center of his menagerie of puppets and animated machinery. After Schlumberger (the last and best of the Turk's hidden operators and chess masters) died of yellow fever after returning from Cuba, Maezel had the Turk installed in the Chinese Museum in Philadelphia. Shortly after, the broken-hearted Maezel died while returning from Cuba by ship to Philadelphia and was buried at sea. For the next nineteen years, the Turk languished largely unattended in the museum until it met its fiery end.

"Babbage Descending into Mt. Vesuvius, 1828" draws heavily on Babbage's own account of his visit to Mt. Vesuvius and his surveying of the dormant and active portions of the volcano's interior. The description of the crater's surface as resembling the blood vessels of the eye comes directly from his memoir. The trip to Europe was part of Babbage's recovery process following his mental breakdown at of 1827.

"Binary" takes its inspiration from the way in which binary numbers are stored in a digital computer as either absence or presence (nothing or something).

"Recursion" opens with a brief nod to Emily Dickinson's line, "Split the lark and you'll find the music."

"Babbage Attempting to Solve for the Unknown" references several phrases from Babbage's economic treatise, *On the Economy of Machinery and Manufactures* (1832) in which he attempts to document and improve upon the efficient processes he discovers in different industries and trades (e.g., scythe factories, wine shipping, rain collection, and water distribution).

"Babbage, Backstage at a Performance of *Don Giovanni,* Finds Himself Caught Between Heaven and Hell" imagines in more intimate detail an experience behind the scenes at the opera as described by Babbage in his memoir, *Passages from the Life of a Philosopher* (1864).

"Free" invokes the memory of poet-artist-critic Weldon Kees and the mysterious circumstances of his disappearance and presumed suicide on July 19, 1955. The abandoned car, the red socks in the sink, and the cat named Lonesome are all details of historical fact. Since his body was never recovered from the San Francisco Bay, some have speculated that he had faked his own death and started over in Mexico.

"Babbage Explaining God and the Machine" is inspired by the frequent presentations Babbage gave in his front parlor using the Beautiful Fragment of the Difference Engine to demonstrate how what is perceived as a miracle (a violation of natural law) might be better understood as the operation of a subroutine, a momentary deviation from the basic law to execute a preplanned set of instructions based on another higher law that contains the lower law's operation. For Babbage, who was a deist, the world and the universe followed a set of rules and patterns, complex at times, but predictable nonetheless. God was the

Divine Programmer, the Earth was His calculating machine, and all nature and phenomena were the output of that grand program.

"Void" uses the // line notation from C++ to indicate that what follows is to be read by the human, but not by the computer (i.e., everything after those marks is to be ignored by the compiler).

"HAL 9000, A Few Moments Before Singing" alludes to the lyrics of "Daisy Bell," the song that HAL sings during its deactivation as it slowly loses its mind.

"Babbage, Circumnavigating the Room, Encounters Ada, 1833" is inspired by the visit of Lady Byron and her then seventeen-year old daughter, Ada, to one of Babbage's famous soirees where he often gave viewings of the Beautiful Fragment and encouraged the mingling of Britain's finest literary, scientific, political, and philosophical minds. It's worth noting that Ada's intuitive grasp of Babbage's work was largely due to Lady Byron's efforts to stamp out any genetic predilection toward wild devilry she might have inherited from her father, the infamous Lord Byron. From a very young age, Ada had been tutored in mathematics and science and kept far from literature and the arts. Thus, when Ada arrived at the party and heard Babbage's discussion of the Difference Engine and his plans for the Analytical Engine, she was well-equipped to appreciate what he was trying to accomplish. However, she did more than appreciate him; it was clear from the beginning that Ada understood what the machine stood for and where Babbage's work was headed. The two, despite a substantial difference in age, soon became very close friends and collaborators. She was instrumental in providing clear translations of contemporary reviews of Babbage's work and insightful and provocative commentary of his plans for the Analytical Engine. Babbage viewed her as a peer; she was one of a very small number who understood the potential of a general-purpose calculating machine and who possessed a vision of its future relevance and application that at times even exceeded his own. At this particular party, Babbage (now a widower) would have made the rounds escorted by his daughter Georgiana who was the same age as Ada and had taken on the role of hostess after her mother's death. Unfortunately, this period of happiness was all too short-lived. Babbage would go on to lose his daughter the following year to illness.

"Babbage Reflecting on the Cruelty of Man, 1835" draws heavily on Babbage's response to an article in *Quarterly Review* (December 1835) describing the actions of a captain of an illegal slaving ship who threw 150 slaves off of his ship along with much of his heavy cargo in an attempt to outrun a British naval ship. Babbage was so incensed by this account and other accounts of the cruelty inflicted on fellow human beings that he expanded his chapter on "The Permanent Impression of Words and Actions on the Globe We Inhabit" in his second edition of *The Ninth Bridgewater Treatise: A Fragment* to include a scathing diatribe against the perpetrators of these murders and others of their ilk. As the title of this chapter suggests, Babbage firmly believed that every utterance and action performed by human beings was recorded permanently in the vibrations of particles in the air, and that in the final judgment of God, all would be judged by this "book" of life.

"Conditional" uses the *if-then-else* conditional structures present is most programming languages.

"Babbage Departing Turin by Coach, 1840" brings together details from Babbage's travels through Europe, most specifically his account of his time in Italy as a guest of the royal court and their chief mathematicians and scholars. Babbage was pleasantly surprised (and a little shocked) to discover that not only were the academics and scholars deeply interested in his work, but the king was, too. Babbage was granted permission to sit in audience with the king and spent considerable time discussing the electric telegraph and other applications of science. All in all, Babbage found himself treated with a level of honor, enthusiasm, and respect to which he was wholly unaccustomed. It was with deep regret that he eventually left Turin and returned home to a country that no longer bore great respect for him or admiration for the work he was doing.

"Deep Blue Confesses" is an imagined letter of apology from supercomputer Deep Blue to world chess champion Gary Kasparov following its defeat of Kasparov in the second game of their 1997 rematch. In his book, *The Signal and The Noise: Why So Many Predictions Fail— But Some Don't,* Nate Silver speculates that Kasparov's loss was actually triggered by his anxiety over Deep Blue's forty-fourth move in the first game—in which the computer had moved its rook for no apparent purpose. Kasparov concluded that the counterintuitive play must be a sign of superior intelligence. He never considered that it was simply a bug.

"Babbage Sending Messages to Ada, Now Gone, 1852" imagines Babbage at his upper window in late fall, days after Ada Lovelace's death from bloodletting (a failed attempt to treat her uterine cancer). The signaling light he operates in the poem is the prototype of the occulting lights he developed just prior to the 1851 Great Exhibition and used to bewilder those returning from the Exhibition. The occulting lights relied on colored lenses and different patterns of obscuring the cast light to communicate coded messages. The system would go on to be adopted by navies and lighthouses around the world. Throughout the Exhibition, Babbage left a box outside his residence for passersby to leave their guesses as to the meaning of that evening's message.

"Return" includes a reference to Babbage's proposed probability calculation for determining the likelihood that a dead man might come back to life. In the context of his argument, this calculation is intended to represent the non-zero likelihood of the resurrection of Jesus Christ. In the context of his life, one can imagine the same thinking in conjunction with his own loved ones.

"Babbage and Carroll in the Silent Workshop, 1867" alludes to the two men's shared interest in cryptography and code-breaking, an intellectual common ground that apparently went undiscovered during their meeting.

"Babbage, Closing His Eyes, 1871" pulls together a number of details from Babbage's life, including his very public feud with street musicians and organ grinders who he saw as public nuisances and extortionists.

"Leviathan Speaks to Babbage at the End" begins with an epigraph from one of Babbage's contemporaries who notes that he often referred to the unbuilt machine as the elusive biblical sea monster mentioned in Job 41:1.

ACKNOWLEDGMENTS

I am grateful to the editors of the following publications, in which these poems, sometimes in slightly different versions, first appeared: *Adroit Journal, American Literary Review, Anti-, The Collagist, The Cossack Review, Dialogist, diode, Eleven Eleven, Exit 7, Iron Horse Literary Review, Kartika Review, Lantern Review, Ninth Letter, The Normal School, Ostrich Review, Radar Poetry, Redactions, RHINO, Stirring, Tayo Literary Magazine, Thrush Poetry Journal,* and *Weave.*

Several of these poems appear in the chapbook *Leviathan* published by Hyacinth Girl Press.

In addition, the following poems appeared in these anthologies: "Conditional" and "Pointer" in *The Loudest Voice: Volume I;* "Free" (as "Things Left Behind") in *Aspects of Robinson: Homage to Weldon Kees;* "Array" in *Don't Blame the Ugly Mug: Ten Years of Two Idiots Peddling Poetry;* "Pointer" and Conditional" in *Fire in the Pasture: Twenty-First Century Mormon Poets;* "Encapsulation," "Float," "Frankenstein's Creature Bids Farewell to Its Maker," "Break," "Operator," and "Long" in *Completely Mixed Up: Mixed Heritage Asian North American Writing and Art.* Also gratitude to the *College Mathematics Journal* for reprinting "Babbage and Carroll in the Silent Workshop" in one of their issues.

Special thanks to my faculty mentors at the University of Southern California who supported me through both the research and the writing of this book, chiefly David St. John, Hilary Schor, and Deborah Harkness, but also Emily Anderson, Rebecca Lemon, Carol Muske-Dukes, and Mark Irwin. Thanks as well to my friends and fellow students in the Ph.D. in Literature and Creative Writing program at USC. I owe a particular debt to Chris Abani and Juan Felipe Herrera whose belief and encouragement of this project in its very early stages while at UC Riverside has finally borne fruit, as well as to Sarah Gambito, Joseph Legaspi, Oliver de la Paz, and the rest of my writing family at Kundiman whose enduring love and powerful words have sustained and inspired me, and to the league of extraordinary writers who engage technology and our relationship to it, namely Margaret Rhee, Jilly Dreadful, Saba Razvi, Noel Pabillo Mariano, Yuzun Kang,

Sydney Padua, Minsoo Kang, Peter Tieryas, and Amaranth Borsuk. I am deeply grateful to Margaret Bashaar for publishing many of the life of Babbage poems in chapbook form as *Leviathan*—her enthusiasm for this project can only be matched by that of Erin Elizabeth Smith, Sara Henning, and the rest of the crew at Sundress Publications.

Thank you to my many writer friends in Los Angeles who have read or heard earlier drafts of these poems at our poetry potlucks and have helped me find my way through them. Much gratitude to Steve Meinel, Matt Versweyveld, Anthony Cuccia, and Thomas Fiola who slogged through the trenches with me day after day during my time as a computer games programmer. Others without whom this book would not be what is: Janalynn Bliss, Brendan Constantine, Allen and Jenny Graves, Mandy Kahn, Douglas Kearney, Grace Lee, Jessica Piazza, Brynn Saito, and Elaine Wang. I remain forever grateful to my late father who brought home early computers from work during the 1980s and bought our first home PC, an IBM PC Jr—the machine I learned to program on. Likewise I owe much to my mother, whose faith in me has never wavered, despite the strangeness of my path; and to my sister whose shared love of programming, games, and science fiction marks us as true siblings, cut from the same cloth. Finally, the impossible and improbable genius of Charles Babbage whose triumphs, sorrows, dreams, and labors were on a scale too great for one lifetime, and yet who nonetheless dared to pursue what no one else could imagine.

ABOUT THE AUTHOR

Neil Aitken is the author of *The Lost Country of Sight* (Anhinga Press), winner of the 2007 Philip Levine Prize, and *Leviathan* (Hyacinth Girl Press), a poetry chapbook. A former computer games programmer and a past Kundiman Poetry Fellow, he holds both an MFA and PhD in creative writing and is the founding editor of *Boxcar Poetry Review*. His poems have appeared in many literary journals and anthologies including *The Adroit Journal, American Literary Review, Crab Orchard Review, diode, Ninth Letter,* and *Southern Poetry Review* . Of Chinese and Scottish heritage, he was born in Vancouver, British Columbia and grew up in Saudi Arabia, Taiwan, and western Canada before moving to the United States for university and work. He lives in Vancouver, Washington.

PRAISE FOR *THE LOST COUNTRY OF SIGHT*

It's difficult to believe that Neil Aitken's **The Lost Country of Sight** is a first book, since there is mastery throughout the collection. His ear is finely tuned, and his capacity for lyricism seems almost boundless. What stands out everywhere in the poems is his imagery, which is not only visually precise but is also possessed of a pure depth. The poems never veer off into the sensational; they are built from pensiveness and quietude and an affection for the world. "Traveling Through the Prairies, I Think of My Father's Voice" strikes me as a perfectly made poem, but poems of similar grace and power are to be found throughout the book. This is a debut to celebrate.

—C.G. Hanzlicek, 2007 Philip Levine Prize Final Judge

Fueled by motion and emotion, Neil Aitken's **The Lost Country of Sight** is literally and figuratively a moving collection. His winding roads and "ghost cars" move us over the landscapes of identity and personal history with stirring meditative grace. "There is a song at the beginning of every journey" Aitken tells us in one poem even as he says in another, "these are journeys we never take." This poet is our both our wise, wide-eyed tour guide and our dazed, day-dreaming companion in *The Lost Country of Sight*. This is a rich, mature debut.

—Terrance Hayes

The voice in these poems is that of a sighted, awake heart discovering its home in language and its homelessness in the world. Steeped in longing, the imagination here is concrete, vivid, sensuous, and ultimately erotic, even as it perceives that meaning and beauty are evanescent.

—Li-Young Lee

OTHER SUNDRESS PUBLICATIONS TITLES

Theater of Parts
M. Mack
$15

Suites for the Modern Dancer
Jill Khoury
$15

Every Love Story is an Apocalypse Story
Donna Vorreyer
$14

What Will Keep Us Alive
Kristin LaTour
$14

Ha Ha Ha Thump
Amorak Huey
$14

Stationed Near the Gateway
Margaret Bashaar
$14

major characters in minor films
Kristy Bowen
$14

Confluence
Sandra Marchetti
$14

Hallelujah for the Ghosties
Melanie Jordan
$14

Fortress
Kristina Marie Darling
$14

When I Wake It Will Be Forever
Virginia Smith Rice
$14

The Lost Animals
David Cazden
$14

A House of Many Windows
Donna Vorreyer
$14

The Hardship Post
Jehanne Dubrow
$14

The Old Cities
Marcel Brouwers
$14

One Perfect Bird
Letitia Trent
$14

Like a Fish
Daniel Crocker
$14

The Bone Folders
T.A. Noonan
$14

CPSIA information can be obtained
at www.ICGtesting.com
Printed in the USA
LVHW031505150821
695369LV00003B/362